Northeast

New Jersey
New York
Pennsylvania

John Ziff

Mason Crest
450 Parkway Drive, Suite D
Broomall, PA 19008
www.masoncrest.com

Printed and bound in the United States of America.

CPSIA Compliance Information: Batch #LES2015.
For further information, contact Mason Crest at 1-866-MCP-Book.

First printing
1 3 5 7 9 8 6 4 2

Library of Congress Cataloging-in-Publication Data

Ziff, John.
  Northeast : New Jersey, New York, Pennsylvania / John Ziff.
    pages cm. — (Let's explore the states)
  Includes bibliographical references and index.
  ISBN 978-1-4222-3329-0
  ISBN 978-1-4222-8614-2
  1. Northeastern States—Juvenile literature. 2. New Jersey—Juvenile literature.
  3. New York—Juvenile literature. 4. Pennsylvania Juvenile literature. I. Title.
  F106.Z54 2015
  974—dc23
                              2014050198

Let's Explore the States series ISBN: 978-1-4222-3319-1

Publisher's Note: Websites listed in this book were active at the time of publication. The publisher is not responsible for websites that have changed their address or discontinued operation since the date of publication. The publisher reviews and updates the websites each time the book is reprinted.

About the Author: John Ziff is an editor and writer. He lives near Philadelphia.

Picture Credits: Architect of the Capitol: 34, 54; The Everett Collection: 40 (center); Independence National Historical Park, Philadelphia: 60 (top); Library of Congress: 14, 15, 16 (bottom), 20 (top left), 31, 32, 35 (top), 36 (top left, bottom left and right), 40 (top), 50, 56 (top left and right); used under license from Shutterstock, Inc.: 5, 6, 10, 12, 13, 24, 25, 27 (bottom left), 28, 36 (top right), 44, 45, 55, 56 (bottom); Andrey Bayda/Shutterstock.com: 41; Dean Bertoncelj/Shutterstock.com: 56 (center); Jon Bilous/Shutterstock.com: 5, 47 (bottom right), 49; Natalia Bratslavsky/Shutterstock.com: 57; S. Bukley/Shutterstock.com: 40 (bottom); Robert Cicchetti/Shutterstock.com: 27 (top); Anthony Correia/Shutterstock.com: 38; Helga Esteb/Shutterstock.com: 20 (top right); Yuguesh Fagoonee/Shutterstock.com: 47 (top); Featureflash/Shutterstock.com: 20 (bottom); Zack Frank/Shutterstock.com: 48; Domenic Gareri/Shutterstock.com: 60 (bottom); Paul Hakimata/Shutterstock.com: 21; Alexandar Iotzov/Shutterstock.com: 33; Ritu Manoj Jethani/Shutterstock.com: 39; Kazela/Shutterstock.com: 29; Andrew F. Kazmierski/Shutterstock.com: 9, 17; Nancy Kennedy/Shutterstock.com: 43; K.L. Kohn/Shutterstock.com: 18 (bottom); Geoffrey Kuchera/Shutterstock.com: 59; Doug Lemke/Shutterstock.com: 47 (bottom left); Maglara/Shutterstock.com: 27 (bottom right); Debra Millet/Shutterstock.com: 35 (bottom); L.E. Mormile/Shutterstock.com: 18 (top); Cristina Muraca/Shutterstock.com: 1; Carrie Nelson/Shutterstock.com: 60 (center); Sean Pavone/Shutterstock.com: 53, 58; Pete Spiro/Shutterstock.com: 19; Ken Tannenbaum/Shutterstock.com: 37; U.S. Navy photo: 16 (top); Spirit of America: 11, 22, 52.

Table of Contents

KEY ICONS TO LOOK FOR:

Words to Understand: These words with their easy-to-understand definitions will increase the reader's understanding of the text, while building vocabulary skills.

Sidebars: This boxed material within the main text allows readers to build knowledge, gain insights, explore possibilities, and broaden their perspectives by weaving together additional information to provide realistic and holistic perspectives.

Research Projects: Readers are pointed toward areas of further inquiry connected to each chapter. Suggestions are provided for projects that encourage deeper research and analysis.

Text-Dependent Questions: These questions send the reader back to the text for more careful attention to the evidence presented there.

Series Glossary of Key Terms: This back-of-the book glossary contains terminology used throughout this series. Words found here increase the reader's ability to read and comprehend higher-level books and articles in this field.

LET'S EXPLORE THE STATES

Atlantic: North Carolina, Virginia, West Virginia

Central Mississippi River Basin: Arkansas, Iowa, Missouri

East South-Central States: Kentucky, Tennessee

Eastern Great Lakes: Indiana, Michigan, Ohio

Gulf States: Alabama, Louisiana, Mississippi

Lower Atlantic: Florida, Georgia, South Carolina

Lower Plains: Kansas, Nebraska

Mid-Atlantic: Delaware, District of Columbia, Maryland

Non-Continental: Alaska, Hawaii

Northern New England: Maine, New Hampshire, Vermont

Northeast: New Jersey, New York, Pennsylvania

Northwest: Idaho, Oregon, Washington

Rocky Mountain: Colorado, Utah, Wyoming

Southern New England: Connecticut, Massachusetts, Rhode Island

Southwest: New Mexico, Oklahoma, Texas

U.S. Territories and Possessions

Upper Plains: Montana, North Dakota, South Dakota

The West: Arizona, California, Nevada

Western Great Lakes: Illinois, Minnesota, Wisconsin

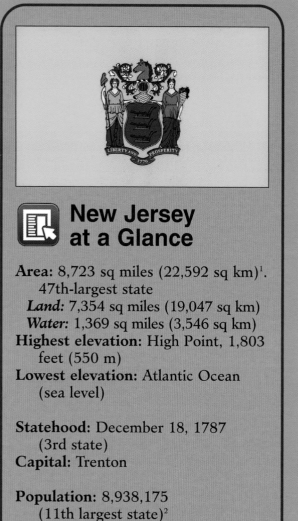

New Jersey at a Glance

Area: 8,723 sq miles (22,592 sq km)[1].
  47th-largest state
  Land: 7,354 sq miles (19,047 sq km)
  Water: 1,369 sq miles (3,546 sq km)
Highest elevation: High Point, 1,803
  feet (550 m)
Lowest elevation: Atlantic Ocean
  (sea level)

Statehood: December 18, 1787
  (3rd state)
Capital: Trenton

Population: 8,938,175
  (11th largest state)[2]

State nickname: the Garden State
State bird: eastern goldfinch
State flower: common meadow violet

[1] *U.S. Census Bureau*
[2] *U.S. Census Bureau, 2014 estimate*

New Jersey

New Jersey is by far the nation's most densely populated state. It's home to nearly 14 times more people per square mile than the United States as a whole.

These facts may call to mind images of crowded cities and sprawling suburban development. New Jersey certainly has its share of those, particularly in the northern part of the state. Yet New Jersey also lives up to its nickname, the Garden State. Survey results released in 2014 by the American Farmland Trust showed New Jersey leading all states in the percentage of farmland protected from development. And the Pinelands National Reserve—a million acres of protected forests, wetlands, and areas of restricted development—stretches across parts of seven southern New Jersey counties.

Geography

New Jersey is located in the eastern United States, along the Atlantic *seaboard*. It has borders with three other states. Delaware is to the southwest. Pennsylvania lies to the west. New York borders New Jersey on the north and, for some 40 miles (64 kilometers), on the east. The rest of eastern New Jersey is bounded by the Atlantic Ocean. New Jersey has about 130 miles (209 km) of coastline.

New Jersey is the fourth smallest state by area. It covers slightly more than 8,720 square miles (22,592 sq km).

Nearly 60 percent of New Jersey's land consists of *coastal plain*. This low-lying, level or gently rolling terrain covers all of southern and part of central New Jersey. Its northern limit runs diagonally across the state, from Raritan Bay in the east to Trenton in the west.

The easternmost part of New Jersey's coastal plain includes salt marshes, *barrier islands*, and sand beaches. Beaches—whether on barrier islands or the mainland—are the pri-

 Words to Understand in This Chapter

barrier island—a long, usually narrow sandy island that runs parallel to the mainland and that was built up through the action of currents and waves.

charter—a grant or guarantee of rights and privileges issued by a ruler or government.

coastal plain—an area of flat, mostly low-lying land that extends inland from a seacoast.

Hessian—a German professional soldier hired by the British to fight in the Revolutionary War.

lords proprietors—persons granted a royal charter to establish and govern a colony in the 1600s.

monopoly—control of a product, resource, or entire market by a single company or individual.

pharmaceutical—a medicinal drug.

piedmont—a gentle slope leading from the base of mountains to a region of flat land.

redistricting—the process of redrawing legislative districts to accommodate changes in population.

seaboard—a region bordering an ocean or sea.

New Jersey is known for its beaches, which are popular with vacationers.

New Jersey is called the "Garden State," because at one time it was known for its fertile farmland. Although today most people think of the state as predominantly urban, many small farms continue to operate, particularly in central New Jersey. Corn and tomatoes are among the notable crops.

mary attraction of the resort communities that line New Jersey's coast. These communities are popular vacation destinations.

Inland, the southern part of the coastal plain is dominated by the Pinelands, also known as the Pine Barrens. Mixed pine and oak forests cover much of the land, which is cut through by numerous creeks and small rivers. The region is sparsely populated. Its soil is too sandy for farming.

To the west of the Pinelands, toward the borders with Delaware and Pennsylvania, New Jersey's coastal plain includes highly productive farmland. Agriculture also flourishes in the northern part of the coastal plain.

North of the coastal plain lies a geographical region called the ***Piedmont***. It's about 20 miles (32 km) wide and contains New Jersey's largest cities. Overall, the Piedmont slopes gradually toward the southeast, but it has some

View of the Delaware Water Gap from Mount Tammany, on the New Jersey side of the river. The Delaware River forms much of the boundary between New Jersey and Pennsylvania.

Water plunges 77 feet (23 m) over the Great Falls of the Passaic River at Paterson, New Jersey. Early Americans used the falling water to power various mills and manufacturing facilities. Since 2009, the Great Falls have been part of a national park.

dramatic features. These include the Watchung Mountains, a series of parallel ridges that are about 40 miles (64 km) long, and the Palisades, sheer cliffs that overlook the western bank of the Hudson River at a height of up to 540 feet (164 meters).

Northwestern New Jersey is a scenic area of mountains, ridges, and valleys. The state's highest elevation, High Point, is in northern Sussex County, near the border with New York. Part of the Kittatinny Mountains, High Point rises more than 1,800 feet (550 m) above sea level.

New Jersey's most important rivers are the Hudson and the Delaware. The Hudson forms the eastern part of New Jersey's border with New York. The Delaware runs the length of New Jersey's western border before emptying into Delaware Bay. Other major rivers include the Passaic (in northern New Jersey) and the Raritan (in the central part of the state).

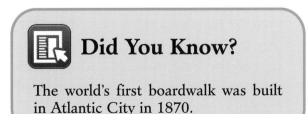

Did You Know?

The world's first boardwalk was built in Atlantic City in 1870.

Every spring, cherry trees bloom in Branch Brook Park, Newark.

New Jersey has few natural lakes. The largest, Lake Hopatcong, covers only four square miles (10 sq km).

New Jersey experiences four distinct seasons. Cold winters and hot summers are the rule. The spring and fall seasons tend to be pleasant. A typical January day in Trenton, situated in the central part of the state, will see a low temperature of about 25° Fahrenheit (–4° Celsius) and a high temperature of around 38°F (3°C). In July, the average daily temperature range is 67° to 85°F (19° to 29°C). Temperatures are lower in the northern part of the state, and higher in the south.

New Jersey receives a moderate amount of precipitation. Statewide, the annual average is about 47 inches (119 cm).

History

The Lenni Lenape, also known as the Delaware Indians, inhabited what is today New Jersey before the arrival of Europeans. Their ancestors had lived in the region since before 7500 BC.

In August 1609, the sea captain Henry Hudson sailed up Delaware Bay and into the Delaware River. The following month, Hudson explored the river that now bears his name. Though he was English, Hudson worked for a Dutch company. He claimed the waters he'd explored, as well as the surrounding territory, for his employer. This territory included what is today New Jersey.

In 1621, the legislature of the Netherlands granted a *charter* to the Dutch West India Company. The charter gave the company a trading *monopoly* in areas of the Western Hemisphere claimed by the Netherlands.

The West India Company soon started the colony of New Netherland. It was centered in what is now New York, with a few outposts in present-day New Jersey.

Over the decades that followed, the Dutch colony expanded slowly. But the Netherlands came into conflict with England, which also had colonies in North America. In 1664, the governor of New Netherland

Henry Hudson was an English sea captain who was hired by the Dutch East India Company to find a westward route to Asia. During his 1609 voyage, he explored the Atlantic coast of New Jersey and traveled up the Hudson River.

surrendered the colony to an English fleet.

England's king, Charles II, awarded New Jersey to his brother, the Duke of York. The duke then sold the land to two men who'd been loyal to the English monarchy. Those men, Sir George Carteret and Lord John Berkeley, were called **lords propri-**

etors. They oversaw the colony under a royal charter but had broad authority to govern as they saw fit. Carteret and Berkeley were progressive in their approach. They permitted religious freedom. They established a constitution. They created a legislative assembly and empowered free males to vote for its members.

Settlers from a wide variety of backgrounds flocked to New Jersey, which Carteret and Berkeley divided into eastern and western provinces. In 1702, their successors transferred governing authority back to the English crown. The two halves of New Jersey were then reunited. For a long time, though, one royal governor was in charge of both the New York and New Jersey colonies. New Jersey rarely received much attention from the governor. In 1738, New Jersey finally got its own governor.

George Washington's December 25, 1776, crossing of the Delaware River and attack on the British garrison at Trenton, New Jersey, was one of the most important Continental Army victories of the American Revolution.

The legend of "Molly Pitcher" originated during the Battle of Monmouth, New Jersey, in June 1778. During the battle, Mary "Molly" Hays helped to load and fire a cannon after her soldier husband was wounded.

New Jersey would play a major role in the Revolutionary War, which broke out in 1775. Many battles were fought on New Jersey soil. None was more important than the Battle of Trenton. If George Washington hadn't defeated a force of **Hessian** soldiers there on December 26, 1776, the Revolution might well have been over. The United States might not have won independence.

The Constitution, which established the U.S. government we know today, was drafted in September 1787. Three months later, New Jersey became the third state to ratify, or approve, the Constitution.

During the 1800s, New Jersey became a major industrial state. Cities such as Paterson, Newark, Jersey City, and Camden flourished as manufacturing centers.

Thomas Edison invented the phonograph, as well as the incandescent light bulb. He helped develop the movie camera and many other inventions at his lab in Menlo Park, New Jersey, and later at a larger research facility in West Orange, New Jersey.

A photo captures the flaming dirigible Hindenburg *as it crashes at Lakehurst, New Jersey, on May 6, 1937. The disaster killed 36 people, and ended the era of the passenger airship.*

New Jersey's population more than doubled, from about 1.9 million to over 4 million, between 1900 and 1940. Immigrants from Europe were largely responsible for this growth. Most settled in North Jersey, which became increasingly urban. South Jersey remains largely rural.

The last decades of the 20th century saw a great deal of development in coastal areas of New Jersey. The risks of building near the ocean were driven home on October 29, 2012. That day, Hurricane Sandy made landfall near Atlantic City. The powerful storm destroyed or damaged more than

Famed aviator Charles Lindbergh testifies during the trial of Bruno Richard Hauptmann, who in 1935 was charged with kidnapping Lindbergh's infant son from his home in Hopewell, New Jersey. The kidnapping and subsequent trial attracted national attention. Hauptmann was found guilty, and was executed in the electric chair in 1936.

In October 2012, Hurricane Sandy caused significant damage throughout New Jersey. The damage was heaviest in towns on the Jersey Shore, such as Belmar, pictured here.

345,000 homes statewide. Total economic losses in New Jersey were estimated at $30 billion.

Government

New Jersey invests more power in the office of governor than does almost any other state. New Jersey's constitution gives the governor authority to appoint the state attorney general, treasurer, secretary of state, and other key officeholders. In most states, these officeholders are elected. New Jersey governors are elected to four-year terms. There is no lifetime limit on the number of terms the same person may

New Jersey governor Chris Christie, elected in 2009, has become a nationally known leader in the Republican Party.

New Jersey's legislature meets in the State House in Trenton, built in 1790.

serve. But governors cannot serve more than two terms in a row.

The New Jersey Legislature is a bicameral (two-chamber) body. The lower chamber is the 80-seat General Assembly. Its members are elected to two-year terms. The upper chamber is the 40-member Senate. Senators are elected to four-year terms, except at the start of a new decade. Then, the senators serve two-year terms. This is to aid in *redistricting*. Members of the New Jersey Legislature aren't limited in the number of terms they may serve.

In addition to its two U.S. senators, New Jersey is allotted 12 seats in the U.S. House of Representatives.

The Economy

Overall, New Jersey is quite prosperous. According to the U.S. Census Bureau, it ranks second among the 50 states in income per person.

Throughout much of the 20th century, manufacturing drove New Jersey's economy. Around 1970, though, the Garden State entered a long period of industrial decline.

Princeton University is consistently ranked among the top five colleges in the United States.

Factory after factory closed, as production was shifted to the American South and West or, later, overseas. New Jersey's experience mirrored that of other old manufacturing states in the Northeast and Midwest. Still, New Jersey has managed to remain a leader in chemical and ***pharmaceutical*** manufacturing. It's also a significant producer of electronics and scientific instruments.

With beaches stretching from Sandy Hook in the north to Cape May in the south, New Jersey is a magnet for vacationers. A recent study found that tourism supports, either directly or indirectly, nearly 10 percent of all jobs in New Jersey. In 2011, tourism directly contributed more than $16 billion to the state's economy.

As far as agriculture is concerned, the Garden State is a leading producer

Some Famous New Jerseyans

Newark-born writer Stephen Crane (1871–1900) is best known for his Civil War novel *The Red Badge of Courage*, though he also wrote short stories and poetry. His writing inspired many American authors of the 20th century.

Bruce Springsteen

Alice Paul (1885–1977), a champion of women's rights, hailed from Mount Laurel.

In a career spanning more than five decades, singer Frank Sinatra (1915–1998), the pride of Hoboken, did it his way.

In July 1969, Essex County native Edwin "Buzz" Aldrin (b. 1930) became the second astronaut to walk on the moon.

Alice Paul

U.S. Supreme Court justices Antonin Scalia (b. 1936) and Samuel Alito (b. 1950) were both born in Trenton. Scalia was appointed to the Court in 1986, while Alito joined the Court in 2006.

Elizabeth native Judy Blume (b. 1938) has captivated millions of young readers with such books as *Tales of a Fourth Grade Nothing*.

Rock legend Bruce Springsteen (b. 1949) was born in Long Branch.

Actress Meryl Streep (b. 1949), a three-time Academy Award winner, got her start in Summit.

Sprinter and long jumper Carl Lewis (b. 1961) was a standout at Willingboro High School before going on to win nine Olympic gold medals.

Jon Stewart (b. 1962) went from class clown in Lawrenceville to professional comedian and host of *The Daily Show*.

Jon Stewart

of cranberries and blueberries. South Jersey's farms grow a variety of vegetables as well. Chickens are also a significant agricultural product of New Jersey.

The People

The 2010 census counted nearly 8.8 million residents of New Jersey—more than 1,195 people per square mile. That's about 15 percent more people per square mile than the next most densely populated state, tiny Rhode Island. With 94.7 percent of its people residing within urban areas, New Jersey trails only California as the most urban state, according to the U.S. Census Bureau.

Racially and ethnically, New Jersey is more diverse than the country as a whole. It has higher percentages of African Americans, Latinos, and Asians. And New Jersey continues to attract immigrants. The latest Census Bureau data show that 12.9 percent of U.S. residents were born outside the United States. The figure for New Jersey is 20.8 percent.

Cape May, a popular beach resort on the southern end of New Jersey, is known for its Victorian-era architecture.

Did You Know?

According to the U.S. Census Bureau, 7 of the 10 most densely populated towns or cities in the country are in New Jersey. With more than 57,000 residents per square mile, the tiny town of Guttenberg, in northern New Jersey's Hudson County, ranks first.

Major Cities

With a population of about 277,000, *Newark* is New Jersey's largest city. It's the county seat of Essex County, in the northeastern part of the state. Newark is a business center and a major transportation hub.

Lower Manhattan (and Wall Street) lies just to the east, across the Hudson River, but *Jersey City* (2010 population: 247,597) is an important financial center in its own right. It's also the seat of Hudson County.

In 1791, *Paterson* was founded near the Great Falls of the Passaic River. The plan was to use the rushing water to power factories, and it worked. Paterson became one of the country's first industrial cities. Today, more than 145,000 people call Paterson home.

Located south of Newark, in Union County, *Elizabeth* is a city of about 125,000. Combined with Port Newark, which it abuts, the Elizabeth Marine Terminal is one of the busiest port facilities in the Northeast.

Historic *Trenton* has served as New Jersey's capital since 1790. Today the city, which is situated along in Delaware River in Mercer County, has a population of nearly 85,000.

Newark is the state's largest city.

Further Reading

Bilby, Joseph G., James M. Madden, and Harry Ziegler. *350 Years of New Jersey History: From Stuyvesant to Sandy*. Charleston, SC: The History Press, 2014.

Doak, Robin. *New Jersey, 1609–1776*. Washington, DC: National Geographic Society, 2005.

Kent, Deborah. *New Jersey*. New York: Scholastic, 2011.

Internet Resources

http://www.state.nj.us/nj/about/history/

This page, from the State of New Jersey, offers links to a variety of interesting historical topics.

http://www.revolutionarywarnewjersey.com/index.htm

This comprehensive online guide to Revolutionary War historic sites in New Jersey includes photos, explanations, and a very detailed timeline.

http://www.visitnj.org/

New Jersey's official state tourism website.

 # Text-Dependent Questions

1. Name the three states that border New Jersey.
2. Which European country claimed New Jersey before England?
3. Which important Revolutionary War battle took place on December 26, 1776?

Research Project

Scientists expect severe storms like Hurricane Sandy to become more common in the coming decades. The reason: global climate change. Find out what climate scientists say is causing the planet to warm, what effects rising temperatures might have, and what can be done to deal with the situation.

New York at a Glance

Area: 54,555 sq miles (141,291 sq km)[1]. 27th largest state
 Land: 47,126 sq mi (122,056 sq km)
 Water: 7,429 sq mi (19,241 sq km)
Highest elevation: Mount Marcy, 5,344 feet (1,629 m)
Lowest elevation: Atlantic Ocean (sea level)

Statehood: July 26, 1788 (11th state)
Capital: Albany

Population: 19,651,127 (3rd largest state)[2]

State nickname: the Empire State
State bird: eastern bluebird
State flower: rose

[1] *U.S. Census Bureau*
[2] *U.S. Census Bureau, 2013 estimate*

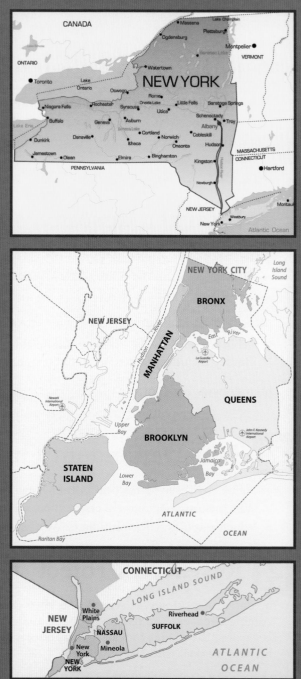

New York

No one knows for certain how New York got its nickname, the Empire State. Some historians point to a letter George Washington wrote to New York City's Common Council. The year was 1785. The Revolutionary War had ended less than two years earlier, and the future of the newly independent United States was unclear. Would the Union survive and prosper?

In his letter, Washington thanked the Common Council for an honor it had recently bestowed on him. He then expressed his hope that "your State (at present the seat of the Empire) may . . . strengthen and give a permanency to the Union at home—and credit and respectability to it abroad."

Whether or not New York's nickname comes from the phrase "the seat of the Empire," one thing does seem clear. The Empire State has more than lived up to Washington's expectations. It played an important role in the rise and expansion of the United States. And, in large part because of New York City, it remains vital in global affairs.

Geography

At more than 54,500 square miles (141,291 sq km), New York is the largest state in the northeastern United States. It has borders with five other states. Vermont, Massachusetts, and Connecticut are to the east. New Jersey and Pennsylvania lie to the south. To the north, New York is bounded by two of the Great Lakes—Erie and Ontario—as well as the Canadian provinces of Ontario and Quebec.

New York's geography is quite diverse. Low, gently sloping or flat terrain hugs the border with Canada and the shores of Lakes Erie and Ontario. Long Island, in the far southeastern part of the state, is also low and flat. In the rest of New York, rugged and dramatic landscapes abound.

Uplands cover much of southern and western New York, extending into the central part of the state. These uplands are the northernmost section of the Allegheny *Plateau*, which also covers parts of Pennsylvania, Ohio, West Virginia, Kentucky, and Tennessee. In New York, the Catskill

Words to Understand in This Chapter

abolitionist—a person who advocated the elimination of slavery.

estuary—an area where ocean tides meet the current of a river or stream, mixing salt water with freshwater.

militia—a group of people who aren't part of the official armed forces of a country but who train for military service in the event of an emergency.

plateau—a large, relatively flat area of land that rises sharply above adjoining land on at least one side.

proclamation—an official public announcement by a government official.

uplands—elevated land at a significant distance from the sea.

Above: Whiteface Mountain is one of the tallest peaks of the Adirondack Mountains, rising 4,865 feet (1,483 m) above sea level.

Right: Even urban centers like New York City contain natural beauty. Central Park covers 843 acres (341 hectares) and is visited by more than 37 million people each year.

View of Niagara Falls from the American side, where water drops more than 165 feet (50 m). Niagara Falls is located on the border between the United States and Canada, and has long been a tourist attraction.

Mountains mark the eastern edge of the plateau. The Catskills' highest peaks top 4,000 feet (1,200 m).

Did You Know?

Algonquin-speaking Indians called the Hudson River *Mohicanituk*, meaning "The River That Flows Both Ways." That's because the lower half of the Hudson is actually a tidal *estuary*. About twice per day, incoming tides from the Atlantic Ocean move northward up the Hudson. These tidal currents reach as far north as Troy.

Another mountain group, the Adirondacks, dominates northeastern New York. At 5,344 feet (1,629 m), Mount Marcy is the tallest peak in the Adirondacks. It's also the highest elevation in the state.

Separating the Adirondacks from the Catskills is the Mohawk Valley. The Mohawk River, which rises in central New York, flows 148 miles (238 km) eastward through the valley. It empties into the Hudson River about nine miles (15 km) north of Albany, New York's capital city.

The south-flowing Hudson is New York's longest river. It rises in the

Adirondacks and runs some 315 miles (507 km) before emptying into Upper New York Bay. Much of the Hudson River valley consists of gently rolling hills. On the west, the valley is bounded by the Catskill Mountains and the Shawangunk Ridge, which is 47 miles (76 km) long. To the east are the foothills of the Taconic Mountains, which form part of New York's border with its New England neighbors.

At its widest, the Hudson River is more than three miles (5 km) across. But the river narrows to as little as a quarter mile in the Hudson Highlands. Along this 15-mile (24-km) stretch, the river cuts through thousand-foot-high mountains. The southernmost part of the Hudson Highlands is about 50 miles (81 km) north of New York City.

A 114-mile (184-km) section of the St. Lawrence River forms part of New York's border with Canada. Other major rivers in New York include the Black, Genesee, and

Fall foliage in the Catskills.

Oswego. All three flow into Lake Ontario.

Nearly 3,000 square miles (7,700 sq km) of Lake Ontario belong to New York. The state also claims more than 590 square miles (1,530 sq km) of Lake Erie. Lake Champlain forms the northern half of New York's border with Vermont. The largest lake entirely within New York is Oneida. Located northeast of Syracuse, in the central part of the state, it covers about 80 square miles (207 sq km).

While all of New York experiences four distinct seasons, conditions vary quite a bit across the state. For example, daily low temperatures for January average 23°F (–5°C) in New York City; 18°F (–8°C) in Buffalo, on the banks of Lake Erie; and just 6°F (–14°C) in Elizabethtown, in the Adirondack region. In a typical year, New York City receives about 25 inches (64 cm) of snow. By contrast, Syracuse, in the central part of the state, averages more than 120 inches (305 cm) of snow, and the Tug Hill area east of Lake Ontario averages 200 inches (508 cm).

With high temperatures frequently reaching the 90s, the New York City area and the Hudson Valley have hotter summers than do upland regions. Overall, rainfall tends to be moderate throughout the state.

History

In 1524, Giovanni da Verrazzano—an Italian in the service of France—explored New York Bay. The upper part of the bay offered an excellent natural harbor. But a century would pass before the first European colonization of the area.

 ### Did You Know?

The Dutch West India Company bought Manhattan Island from a group of Indians, probably Lenni Lenape, in 1626. The purchase price was trade goods worth 60 guilders, or about $1,000 in today's money. Most historians believe that the Dutch and the Indians had a different understanding of what the deal meant. Native Americans didn't think of land as something that individuals could own.

During his 1609 voyage on behalf of a Dutch commercial company, Henry Hudson sailed into the Hudson River. Hudson followed the river north for some 135 miles (217 km). Near the site of present-day Albany, the water became too shallow for his ship to proceed further. The river and the Hudson Valley were part of the vast territory Hudson claimed for his employer.

Dutch merchants were soon plying the Hudson (which they called the North River). They traded with Lenni Lenape and Mahican (also spelled Mohican) peoples. The Indians received items such as metal tools and cloth. The merchants received animal furs, which were highly valued in Europe at the time.

Officials in the Netherlands wanted to establish a permanent Dutch presence in North America. But by itself, the fur trade failed to spur colonization. So in 1621, the Netherlands' legislature chartered the Dutch West India Company. The company was granted a 24-year trade monopoly in America, as well as in Africa. In return, it was expected to colonize Dutch-claimed territory in America.

This painting depicts Dutch ships arriving at the colony of New Amsterdam in the 1640s.

The New Netherland colony's first settlers arrived in 1624. The original plan was to spread colonists across the entire territory claimed by the Netherlands, with settlements in present-day southeastern Pennsylvania, New Jersey, New York, and Connecticut. Within a few years, however, the colony had a clear center: New Amsterdam. It was situated at the southern end of Manhattan Island.

New Amsterdam, and the rest of the New Netherland colony, slowly grew. But English colonization of the region was also expanding. By the 1640s, English settlements dotted eastern Long Island.

Eventually, England and the Netherlands came into conflict. In September 1664, an English fleet forced the surrender of New Amsterdam and Fort Orange, at the site of Albany. Having taken New Netherland's capital, and with control of the strategic Hudson River, England claimed the entire colony, which was renamed New York. New Amsterdam became New York City.

In 1673, the Dutch regained their colony during a war with England. But

Residents of the Dutch New Amsterdam colony ask governor Peter Stuyvesant not to fire on British warships that have arrived in 1664 to claim the territory for England. Stuyvesant, who governed the colony from 1647 until 1664, had a major influence on the growth and development of New York City. He surrendered the colony to the British in September 1664.

the following year, in the treaty that ended the war, they permanently gave up all claims to the colony.

In the decades that followed, England would come into increasing conflict with another colonial rival: France. The two nations fought a series of wars. Violence often erupted between French and British colonists in North America.

By the mid-1700s, France claimed a huge swath of territory in North America. It ran through the interior of the continent, from Canada all the way to the Gulf of Mexico. While most British colonists still lived within 50 or 60 miles of the Atlantic coast, there was growing pressure in the 13 colonies to expand westward.

In 1754, a dispute over control of the Ohio River valley touched off a huge conflict, with battlefields around the globe. In North America, the conflict would be called the French and Indian War. It pitted British regular soldiers, British colonial *militias*, and allied Indians such as the Iroquois against French soldiers, French colonial militias, and Indians such as the

The Iroquois people of western New York lived in longhouses like this one. Six Native American tribes worked together in an alliance known as the Iroquois Confederacy.

Algonquin. A couple major battles took place in what is now upstate New York. By 1763, the British forces had won. France gave up its claims to territory east of the Mississippi River.

But the seeds of another conflict were quickly sown. Great Britain's king, George III, issued a *proclamation* that prohibited westward expansion of the American colonies. Also, Britain's parliament imposed new taxes on the colonists. Relations between the British government and

British general John Burgoyne surrenders his army at Saratoga, New York, October 1777. The Battle of Saratoga was a crucial victory for the Continental Army during the Revolution. News of the victory encouraged France, Britain's greatest rival, to enter the conflict on the American side. The French provided weapons and other supplies, as well as troops to fight the British.

the colonists grew steadily worse. Finally, in 1775, the Revolutionary War broke out.

New York was the scene of many battles. The Battle of Long Island, which involved more than 40,000 men in all, was the war's largest single engagement. Fought on August 27, 1776, it was a British victory. Less than a month later, the British took New York City, which they would occupy until the end of the war. But on October 7, 1777, the Americans won a huge victory in the northern Hudson Valley. The Battle of Saratoga not only stopped a British invasion force from Canada, but also helped convince France to support the American cause.

On July 26, 1788, New York became the 11th state to ratify the U.S. Constitution. The following year, New York City became the first federal capital under the Constitution. Although the capital was moved to Philadelphia in 1790, New York's importance grew steadily in the decades that followed. By 1810, New York had surpassed Virginia as the state with the largest population.

New York City, meanwhile, became the country's biggest center of commerce and trade. That position was solidified with the construction of the Erie Canal. Completed in 1825, the 363-mile (584-km) waterway connected the Hudson River with Lake Erie. This enabled goods and people to move with relative ease between New York Harbor and the Midwest. Towns sprang up all around the Erie Canal. The construction of other canals, railroads,

Alexander Hamilton was an important political figure in the early history of the United States. He was instrumental in gaining state approval of the U.S. Constitution, the basis for America's current system of government, and also helped to set up a strong financial system for the new country.

A lock on the Erie Canal near Clay, New York. Construction of the Erie Canal in the early 19th century contributed to the settlement of western New York State, and also helped make New York City the country's most important seaport.

Between 1892 and 1954, more than 12 million immigrants landed at New York Harbor, seeking new lives in the United States.

The Brooklyn Bridge, the first steel-wire suspension bridge, was considered an engineering marvel when it opened in 1883. Today it is a cultural icon of New York.

In 1901, President William McKinley was assassinated while attending an event in Buffalo. His vice president, New Yorker Theodore Roosevelt, assumed the presidency.

Stars like Babe Ruth (back row, center) and Lou Gehrig (back, fourth from right) helped the New York Yankees win many championships during the 1920s and 1930s.

and, a bit later, turnpikes further spurred economic growth in the state.

The promise of economic opportunity made New York a magnet for immigrants throughout the 19th and 20th centuries. That remains the case today. According to the U.S. Census Bureau, only California has more foreign-born residents than New York.

New York City's status as the country's financial capital was a primary reason the terrorist group al-Qaeda targeted it. On September 11, 2001, al-Qaeda terrorists flew two hijacked airliners into the twin towers of New York's World Trade Center. The attack claimed nearly 3,000 lives.

On September 11, 2001, terrorists struck at America's financial center by flying hijacked airliners into the twin towers of the World Trade Center in Manhattan. The attacks launched the United States into wars in Afghanistan and Iraq.

Government

The New York State Legislature is a bicameral body. The lower chamber is the 150-seat Assembly. Under New York's state constitution, the number of seats in the upper chamber, the Senate, can vary. As of 2014, New York had 63 state senate districts. Senators and members of the Assembly are elected to two-year terms. There are no limits on the number of terms an individual may serve.

New Yorkers elect their governor every four years. No term limits apply.

In the U.S. Congress, New York has 27 members of the House of Representatives. Twenty-one of them, in addition to both of New York's U.S. senators, were Democrats as of 2014.

The Economy

New York has a huge economy. In 2012, the total value of goods and services produced in the state was estimated at about $1.2 trillion—more than all but 13 countries.

It would be hard to overstate the importance of banking and finance to New York's economy. As of 2013, the five largest investment banks in the world were all headquartered in New York City. So, also, are the world's two largest stock exchanges, the New York Stock Exchange and NASDAQ.

New York City is a major center for publishing. All of the country's major broadcast television networks, and many large cable TV channels, are headquartered in New York City as well.

Chemicals, electrical equipment, and scientific instruments are among New York State's leading manufactured products. Agricultural production is centered in the Mohawk and Hudson valleys.

Visitors to the Empire State spent more than $57 billion in 2012. Nearly

A statue of George Washington watches over the New York Stock Exchange building on Wall Street in New York City. The city is one of the world's most important centers of banking and finance.

The city of Albany in western New York has been the state capital since 1797. The city originated in 1614, when Dutch colonists built a fort on the site. This makes Albany one of the oldest continuously inhabited European settlements in the United States.

715,000 New Yorkers work in jobs that are supported by the tourism industry.

The People

New York is the country's third largest state by population. The Empire State has more than 19.6 million residents.

New York's population is diverse. Compared with the United States as a whole, New York has a significantly smaller proportion of whites, and larger proportions of African Americans, Latinos, and Asians. And over the past two decades, New York's Asian and Latino communities have been growing at rapid rates.

The Empire State's racial and ethnic diversity is largely attributable to New York City, which attracts people from all over the world. Upstate New York has a higher percentage of white people, and smaller percentages of minorities, than the United States overall.

Major Cities

More than 8.3 million people live in *New York City*, making the Big Apple, as it's nicknamed, the largest city in

Some Famous New Yorkers

Presidents Martin Van Buren (1782–1862), Millard Fillmore (1800–1874), Chester A. Arthur (1829–1886), Grover Cleveland (1837–1908), Theodore Roosevelt (1858–1919), and Franklin D. Roosevelt (1882–1945) all grew up in the Empire State.

You might be familiar with the stories "Rip Van Winkle" and "The Legend of Sleepy Hollow." Both were created by New York writer Washington Irving (1783–1859).

Franklin D. Roosevelt

Walt Whitman (1819–1892), considered one of America's most important poets, was born and raised on Long Island.

Poet, women's rights advocate, and *abolitionist* Julia Ward Howe (1819–1910), a native of New York City, penned "The Battle Hymn of the Republic," a popular song of the Civil War era.

A short list of Hollywood heavyweights who hail from New York would include directors Woody Allen (b. 1935) and Martin Scorsese (b. 1942) and actors Al Pacino (b. 1940), Robert De Niro (b. 1943), Robert Downey Jr. (b. 1965), and Scarlett Johansson (b. 1984)

The comedian Jerry Seinfeld (b. 1954) was born in Brooklyn and grew up on Long Island. He is best known for creating the TV sitcom *Seinfeld*, which ran from 1989 to 1998 and was set in Manhattan's Upper West Side.

Jerry Seinfeld

The playgrounds of New York City have produced many basketball stars, including the NBA's all-time leading scorer, Kareem Abdul-Jabbar (1947–   ).

New York City, the birthplace of hip-hop, nurtured such talents as Russell Simmons (b. 1957), Jay-Z (b. 1969), 50 Cent (b. 1975), Tupac Shakur (1971–1996), and Biggie Smalls (1972–1997).

Jay-Z

Singer-songwriter Lady Gaga (b. 1986) is a lifelong resident of Manhattan.

the United States. New York covers 303 square miles (785 sq km) and is made up of five boroughs: The Bronx, Brooklyn, Manhattan, Queens, and Staten Island. It's a place of astonishing cultural diversity, where virtually every nationality is represented and 800 languages are spoken. New York is home to the United Nations' headquarters. It's home to Wall Street, one of the world's leading financial centers. New York is a paradise for lovers of the fine arts, dance, theater, and music. Other attractions include such iconic American landmarks as the Statue of Liberty, Ellis Island, Central Park, and the Brooklyn Bridge.

Located on the eastern shore of Lake Erie, *Buffalo* once thrived as a shipping hub and center of heavy industry. It still has the country's busiest inland port, but Buffalo's

The busy intersection at Times Square in Lower Manhattan.

industrial base has suffered a long decline. So, too, has its population, from a peak of more than 580,000 in 1950 to about 260,000 today.

More than 210,000 people live in *Rochester*. It's located south of Lake Ontario, in Monroe County.

Yonkers (population: 195,976) is situated on the eastern banks of the Hudson River, in Westchester County.

It borders The Bronx and is sometimes jokingly referred to as New York City's sixth borough.

About 145,000 people call *Syracuse* home. It's the county seat of central New York's Onondaga County.

Albany has been New York's capital city since 1797. The 2010 U.S. census counted 97,856 residents.

Further Reading

Burgan, Michael. *New York, 1609–1776*. Washington, DC: National Geographic Society, 2006.

Kyi, Tanya Lloyd. *New York City*. Toronto: Whitecap Books Ltd., 2010.

Somervil, Barbara A. *New York*. New York: Scholastic, 2011.

Internet Resources

http://www.dos.ny.gov/kids_room/

Fun and informative resources for young students, from New York's Department of State.

http://www.iloveny.com/things-to-do/history/timeline/

This timeline of New York history includes photographs and links to places of interest.

http://www.eriecanalway.org/documents/07-2_National_Significance_Final.pdf

An in-depth examination of the Erie Canal.

Text-Dependent Questions

1. By what nickname is New York State known?
2. Which two bodies of water did the Erie Canal connect?
3. How many U.S. presidents from New York can you name?

Research Project

Between 1892 and 1954, more than 12 million immigrants to the United States passed through the Ellis Island immigration station in Upper New York Bay. Investigate your family history. Ask your parents, grandparents, or other relatives what they know about your ancestors. When did your ancestors first arrive in America? Which country or countries did they come from? Using the information you find out, make a family tree. For each person on your family tree, try to include the year and place of the person's birth (and, if applicable, death). Also include, if you know it, the person's occupation and a brief summary of any family stories about him or her. If any of your ancestors passed through Ellis Island, you can search for records at:

www.ellisisland.org/search/passSearch.asp

Scenic view of the Hudson River valley at the Bear Mountain Bridge. The small peak on the left is known as Anthony's Nose.

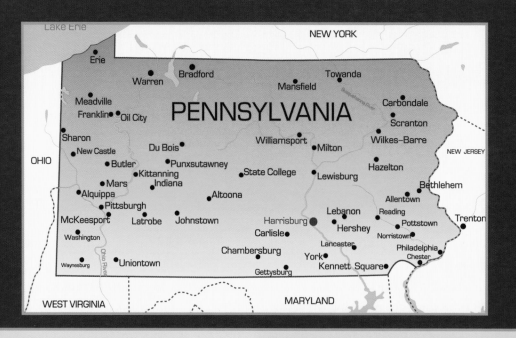

Pennsylvania at a Glance

Area: 46,054 sq miles
(119,280 sq km)[1]. 33rd largest state
Land: 44,743 sq mi (115,884 sq km)
Water: 1,311 sq mi (3,396 sq km)
Highest elevation: Mount Davis,
3,213 feet (979 m)
Lowest elevation: Delaware River at
border with Delaware (sea level)

Statehood: December 12, 1787
(2nd state)
Capital: Harrisburg

Population: 12,773,801
(6th largest state)[2]

State nickname: the Keystone State
State bird: ruffed grouse
State flower: mountain laurel

[1] *U.S. Census Bureau*
[2] *U.S. Census Bureau, 2013 estimate*

Pennsylvania

Pennsylvania has been the scene of some of the most pivotal events in the nation's history. It's where the 13 colonies declared their independence from Great Britain. It's where the *Founding Fathers* hammered out a blueprint for replacing a struggling government with "a more perfect Union." And it's where a great turning point occurred when the Union faced its most severe test.

Geography

At just over 46,000 square miles (119,000 sq km), Pennsylvania is the 33rd largest state by total area. It has borders with six other states. New York is to the north, and New Jersey to the east. Delaware lies to the southeast. Maryland forms most of Pennsylvania's southern border, with West Virginia wrapping around the southwestern corner of the state. Ohio is to the west. Northwestern Pennsylvania is bounded by Lake Erie.

Southeastern Pennsylvania is a lowland area, though the region is hilly in places.

Most of the rest of the state is covered by mountains, valleys, ridges, and plateaus. The Appalachians sweep across central Pennsylvania, running in a northeasterly direction. The Allegheny Mountains, which form the western part of the Appalachians in Pennsylvania, contain the state's highest elevations. At 3,213 feet (979 m) above sea level, Mount Davis is Pennsylvania's highest point. It's located in Somerset County, near the Maryland border.

North and west of the Allegheny Mountains is the Allegheny Plateau. The plateau gives way to a narrow band of lowlands along the shoreline of Lake Erie.

Pennsylvania's major rivers include the Delaware, which forms the state's eastern border. The Susquehanna, which rises in New York, meanders through east-central Pennsylvania before crossing into Maryland and

Words to Understand in This Chapter

allegiance—loyalty owed by a citizen to his or her government.

delegate—a representative to a convention or conference.

Founding Fathers—broadly, the generation of leaders who established the United States by signing the Declaration of Independence, fighting in the Revolutionary War, and drafting the U.S. Constitution.

latitude—distance north or south of the equator, measured in degrees (up to 90 degrees).

philanthropist—a person who donates large sums of money to make life better for other people.

Quaker—a member of the Religious Society of Friends, a Christian sect founded in England in the mid-1600s.

veto—to refuse to sign legislation to prevent its enactment; an instance of rejecting legislation by a president, governor, or other official with executive powers.

Located in Tioga and Lycoming counties, the Pine Creek Gorge is known as the "Grand Canyon of Pennsylvania." It has a maximum depth of 1,450 feet (442 m). A portion of the gorge was designated was designated a National Natural Landmark in 1968.

Sunset over the Susquehanna River, which flows through Pennsylvania to the Chesapeake Bay.

The first American lighthouse on the Great Lakes was built at Presque Island, near Erie, in 1818. This lighthouse replaced it in 1872.

The view from atop Hawk Mountain, part of the Blue Ridge Mountain chain of the Appalachians that runs through east-central Pennsylvania. Hawk Mountain is home to a large wild bird refuge where migratory eagles, hawks, and falcons spend time each year.

emptying into Chesapeake Bay. The south-flowing Allegheny River cuts across western Pennsylvania, uniting with the north-flowing Monongahela

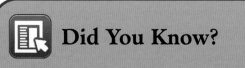

Did You Know?

The first commercial oil well in the United States was drilled in northwestern Pennsylvania. On August 27, 1859, the Drake Well, near the borough of Titusville, struck oil at a depth of more than 69 feet.

at Pittsburgh to form the Ohio River. The Ohio flows northwest into the state of Ohio.

A total of 735 square miles (1904 sq km) of Lake Erie belongs to Pennsylvania. But the state has no other large natural lakes. The biggest, Conneaut Lake, covers less than 1.5 square miles (3.9 sq km). The largest man-made lake entirely within Pennsylvania is 13-square-mile (34-sq-km) Raystown Lake. It's located in Huntington County, in the south-central part of the state.

All of Pennsylvania experiences

Western and central Pennsylvania tend to receive more snow than the eastern part of the state.

four distinct seasons. However, climatic conditions vary considerably by region. Higher-elevation areas in the western and northern parts of the state have longer, colder winters with more snowfall than does southeastern Pennsylvania. For example, on a typical January day in Bradford, in northern Pennsylvania's McKean County, the thermometer never rises above the freezing mark. The average daily range is 12° to 30°F (−11° to −1°C). Philadelphia, by contrast, experiences average January lows of 26°F (−3°C), and average highs of 40°F (4°C). And Philadelphia's average annual snowfall is less than one-third of Bradford's 72 inches (183 cm). Summers tend to be hottest in southeastern Pennsylvania. Philadelphia's average July high temperature is 87°F (31°C). That's 4°F warmer than the average in

Pittsburgh, for example, and 7°F warmer than the average for Erie. Statewide, annual precipitation in Pennsylvania averages about 41 inches (104 cm).

History

European settlement in what is today Pennsylvania dates to the early 1640s. At that time, Swedes and Finns established scattered communities along or near the Delaware River as part of a short-lived Swedish colony called New Sweden. In 1655, a Dutch military expedition forced the colony's surren-

der. The land was part of the territory claimed by New Netherland.

But large-scale colonization really began with the English. In 1681, England's king, Charles II, granted to William Penn a charter for land west of New Jersey, north of Maryland, and south of New York. In all, it included more than 40,000 square miles (103,600 sq km). The land grant settled a debt the Crown had owed to Penn's father, an admiral.

William Penn belonged to the Religious Society of Friends. The **Quakers**, as they were commonly

William Penn arrives at the Pennsylvania colony in 1699, meeting both colonists and Native Americans at the dock some 15 years after his previous visit. One of Penn's greatest accomplishments was writing the "Charter of Privileges," which granted religious freedom to residents of the colony. He also established the framework for a democratic government in which members of the general assembly were elected by the people.

known, refused to accept the authority of the official Church of England. They also refused to swear an oath of *allegiance* to the Crown. The Quakers believed that a person's behavior should be dictated only by his or her conscience. The "Inward Light" of God, they said, resided within everyone. For these, and for other beliefs and practices, the Quakers were harassed and persecuted. Penn himself was imprisoned several times.

Penn's royal charter gave him near-total authority in his colony. But he had something different in mind. He thought people should participate in their own government. He wanted his colony to be a "holy experiment" in religious tolerance, fairness, and "brotherly love." Although the king had given him legal title to Pennsylvania (meaning "Penn's woods"), Penn insisted on paying the Lenni Lenape Indians for all land on which colonists settled.

Penn had visionary ideas. He sometimes didn't pay enough attention to details, however. The royal charter fixed Pennsylvania's southern

Did You Know?

Tradition holds that the Liberty Bell was rung on July 8, 1776, to summon Philadelphians to the first public reading of the Declaration of Independence. The bell was originally made to commemorate the 50th anniversary of William Penn's Charter of Privileges.

boundary at 40°N. But Penn failed to take the basic step of locating that line of *latitude*, which also marked Maryland's northern border. As a result, he promoted settlement on land that rightfully belonged to Maryland. This included Philadelphia, the new city Penn laid out to serve as Pennsylvania's capital.

All this would have been bad enough in the view of Lord Baltimore, the proprietor of the Maryland colony. But Penn also petitioned the king for—and was granted—land that makes up the present-day state of Delaware. Called the Lower Counties, it would officially remain part of Pennsylvania until 1776. Lord

Marker set by the surveyors Charles Mason and Jeremiah Dixon to mark the boundary between Pennsylvania and Maryland. Mason and Dixon conducted their survey between 1763 and 1767. Since then, the Mason-Dixon Line has often been used to make a distinctions between Northern and Southern states.

Baltimore thought this territory was his. Border disputes between Pennsylvania and Maryland wouldn't be resolved until the 1760s, with the drawing of the Mason-Dixon Line.

Inside Pennsylvania, the early years of the colony didn't exactly fulfill Penn's vision of a society based on "brotherly love." Quakers feuded with non-Quakers. Disputes simmered over land, control of trade, and the powers Penn had retained for himself as governor versus those he'd given to the elected legislature. The problems were made worse by Penn's long absences from the colony. He was in Pennsylvania only from 1682 to 1684 and from 1699 to 1701.

Despite this, Penn left a hugely important legacy: the Charter of Privileges. Issued in 1701, it would serve as Pennsylvania's constitution for 75 years. The charter established a single-chamber legislature, the Assembly. All free adult men—not just landowners, as was the case in other colonies—had the right to vote for its members. The Assembly was given sole power to make laws. The gover-

Philadelphia remains among the largest cities in the U.S., with a population of more than 1.5 million.

nor could **veto** legislation. But, critically, the governor couldn't dissolve the Assembly if he found himself at loggerheads with it. The Charter of Privileges also guaranteed freedom of religion, and a broad range of other rights, in Pennsylvania. No other colony had a higher level of democracy or individual liberty.

Throughout the 1700s, immigrants from Europe flocked to Pennsylvania. Many came for religious freedom. By 1770, Pennsylvania's population stood at about 240,000. Among the colonies, only Virginia had more people.

Relations between Great Britain and the colonies grew steadily worse during the early 1770s. Historically, the 13 colonies had relatively little experience working together. Often, they saw themselves as rivals.

But in September 1774, the colonies sent representatives to a meeting, hoping to present a unified front to the British. They chose Philadelphia as the site of the First

Members of the Second Continental Congress wrote and adopted the Declaration of Independence in the Pennsylvania State House in Philadelphia during the summer of 1776.

Continental Congress. Philadelphia was the largest city in the colonies, and Pennsylvania was centrally located—a possible explanation for its nickname, the Keystone State. The First Continental Congress adjourned in October 1774 after issuing a statement outlining the colonies' grievances against the British government.

The Second Continental Congress convened in Philadelphia in May 1775. A few weeks before, Massachusetts colonists had fought British soldiers at Lexington and Concord. Yet many American colonists held out hope that their dif-ferences with the British government could still be patched up. Any chance for reconciliation was ended forever on July 4, 1776. That day, the Continental Congress officially adopt-ed the Declaration of Independence.

On September 11, 1777, British forces defeated the Continental Army at the Battle of Brandywine. That opened the way to Philadelphia, which the British occupied two weeks later. The Continental Congress fled, even-tually ending up in York, Pennsylvania.

During the winter of 1777–1778, the Continental Army encamped at Valley Forge, about 25 miles (40 km) northwest of Philadelphia. Conditions were difficult. Food was often scarce, and many of the soldiers lacked warm clothing. But, as a result of intense training at Valley Forge, George Washington's troops grew much more disciplined and effective as a fighting force. The British would discover this after they abandoned Philadelphia in June 1778.

In 1783, Great Britain officially recognized American independence after being defeated in the Revolutionary War. At the time, the United States operated under a constitution called the Articles of Confederation. It gave nearly all governing power to the individual states. They functioned almost like 13 independent nations. The central government was very weak.

The country faltered. Economic chaos reigned, as each state set its own trade policies and printed its own money. A rebellion broke out in Massachusetts in 1786. But there was no national army to help put down the rebels.

In 1787, *delegates* from every state except Rhode Island traveled to Philadelphia to attend the Constitutional Convention. Its purpose was to fix the problems created by the Articles of Confederation. The

The Continental Army spent the winter of 1777–78 in small cabins like these at Valley Forge, to the northwest of Philadelphia. The area is now a national park. The army struggled to survive at Valley Forge due to shortages of food and warm clothing. However, training the troops received during this period prepared them to fight the powerful British army to a stalemate in the northern colonies over the next two years.

The first fully electronic computer, ENIAC, was built at the University of Pennsylvania. Finished in 1946, the machine took up several rooms and weighed more than 30 tons.

Union troops repulse Pickett's Charge during the third day of the Battle of Gettysburg. Many people believe the Confederate defeat at Gettysburg marked the turning point in the Civil War.

The Pittsburgh Steelers football team has won six Super Bowl titles, more than any other NFL team.

In March 1979, America's worst commercial nuclear accident occurred at the Three Mile Island plant in central Pennsylvania. The accidental loss of cooling water in one of the four reactor towers nearly caused a disastrous meltdown of the reactor core. Radioactive water and gases were vented from the plant, forcing thousands of people to evacuate the area.

delegates eventually drew up an entirely new constitution. The Constitution of the United States created a strong federal government. It spread power carefully across the legislative, executive, and judicial branches of government. On December 12, 1787, Pennsylvania became the second state to ratify the Constitution.

One issue the Founding Fathers failed to address was slavery. It increasingly divided the northern and southern states as the 1800s progressed. Finally, in 1861, the Civil War broke out. The war's bloodiest battle was fought July 1–3, 1863, at Gettysburg, Pennsylvania. The Union victory was a major turning point in the war.

Government

Pennsylvania's legislature, the General Assembly, consists of the 203-seat House of Representatives and the 50-seat Senate. Members of the House are elected to two-year terms. Senators serve for four years. There are no term limits on legislators.

Pennsylvanians elect their governor every four years. Governors are limited to two consecutive terms.

State government buildings in Harrisburg, the capital of Pennsylvania.

Once known for steel mills, Pittsburgh has become home to many technology-related industries.

Pennsylvania's delegation to the U.S. Congress includes 18 members of the House of Representatives, in addition to two U.S. senators.

The Economy

Pennsylvania was once a leading manufacturing center. In the early 1900s, Pittsburgh alone accounted for about half of the country's steel production. Factories in Philadelphia produced a wide range of goods, but especially textiles and clothing. Like other states in the Northeast and Midwest, Pennsylvania's manufacturing sector declined dramatically in the last half of the 20th century. But factories in the Keystone State still churn out such products as fabricated metals, chemicals, plastics, and glassware.

Rich coal deposits in northeastern and western Pennsylvania, as well as oil in the western part of the state, made Pennsylvania the country's top fossil-fuel producer in the late 1800s and early 1900s. In the early 21st century, Pennsylvania has seen a boom in the production of another energy source: natural gas. It's abundant in the Marcellus shale formation, which covers northern and western Pennsylvania. The gas is extracted through a process called hydraulic fracturing, or fracking. Critics of fracking worry about its possible environmental impacts, including contamination of groundwater. But the shale-gas industry has brought tens of thousands of jobs to Pennsylvania.

Pennsylvania has excellent farmland, particularly in the southeastern part of the state. Leading crops include corn, wheat, hay, and mushrooms. Dairy and livestock production are also vital parts of Pennsylvania's agricultural sector.

Among the most important parts of Pennsylvania's service sector are health care and financial services. Philadelphia and Pittsburgh lead in these fields.

An Amish farm in Lancaster County, Pennsylvania. The Amish—sometimes called "Pennsylvania Dutch"—are descended from members of a religious sect that came to Pennsylvania in the 1700s, seeking religious freedom. The Amish shun many modern conveniences.

Some Famous Pennsylvanians

A printer, publisher, author, scientist, inventor, diplomat, and patriot, Benjamin Franklin (1706–1790) was Philadelphia's leading citizen. He helped establish the nation's first hospital, first successful fire insurance company, and first subscription library—all of them in Philadelphia.

James Buchanan (1791–1868) is the only Pennsylvanian to become president of the United States, as well as the only bachelor to serve as president.

You might not have heard of businessman and *philanthropist* Milton Hershey (1857–1945), but you've probably tasted some of the sweet products of the chocolate company he founded.

Benjamin Franklin

Uniontown native George C. Marshall (1880–1959) was a four-star general, secretary of defense, and secretary of state. He won a Nobel Peace Prize for a plan he devised to rebuild Europe after World War II.

Kobe Bryant

Western Pennsylvania has produced some of the NFL's greatest quarterbacks, including Hall of Fame members Johnny Unitas (1933–2002), Joe Namath (b. 1943), Joe Montana (b. 1956), Jim Kelly (b. 1960), and Dan Marino (b. 1961).

Taylor Swift

Philadelphia's Wilt Chamberlain (1936–1999) and Lower Merion's Kobe Bryant (b. 1978) are among the basketball legends from the Keystone State. Both scored more than 31,000 points in the NBA.

Comedian and actress Tina Fey (b. 1970) hails from Upper Darby.

Singer Taylor Swift (b. 1989) grew up in Wyomissing.

The People

"Pennsylvania," a political consultant once observed, "is Philadelphia and Pittsburgh, with Alabama in between." What he meant is that, outside of the Keystone State's two largest metropolitan areas, Pennsylvanians tend to be rather conservative.

The U.S. Census Bureau estimates more than 12.7 million residents of the Keystone State in 2014, making Pennsylvania larger than all but five other states. Racially, Pennsylvania is somewhat less diverse than the country as a whole. According to the U.S. Census Bureau, non-Hispanic whites account for 78.8 percent of Pennsylvania's population. That's nearly 16 percent higher than the figure for the United States overall. Pennsylvania has smaller proportions of all major minority groups tracked by the Census Bureau.

Major Cities

As the birthplace of both the Declaration of Independence and the U.S. Constitution, *Philadelphia* played a unique role in the early history of the United States. The City of Brotherly Love remains one of the country's great urban centers. It features a multitude of historic and cultural attractions, as well as one of the largest urban park systems in the world. With a resident population of more than 1.5 million, Philadelphia is the nation's fifth largest city.

More than 305,000 people call *Pittsburgh* home. It's located in western Pennsylvania, at the confluence of the Allegheny, Monongahela, and Ohio rivers. The heavy industry that once drove Pittsburgh's economy is largely gone, but the Steel City has successfully remade itself as a center for health care, life sciences, and related industries.

Located in eastern Pennsylvania's Lehigh County, *Allentown* is a city of more than 118,000.

Erie is a port city on Lake Erie. It's home to about 101,000 people.

Harrisburg is Pennsylvania's capital city. Located in Dauphin County, in the south-central part of the state, it has a population of close to 50,000.

Further Reading

Hasan, Heather. *Pennsylvania*. New York: Rosen Publishing Group, 2009.

Meredith, Frank, editor. *The Battle of Gettysburg as Seen by Two Teens: The Stories of Tillie Pierce and Daniel Skelly*. Schoharie, NY: Savannah Books, 2010.

Trumbauer, Lisa. *Pennsylvania, 1643–1776*. Washington, DC: National Geographic Society, 2005.

Internet Resources

http://www.portal.state.pa.us/portal/server.pt/community/pennsylvania_history/4276

The website of the Pennsylvania Historical & Museum Commission offers short biographies, articles about important events, and much more.

http://www.ushistory.org/tour/index.html

Take a virtual tour of Philadelphia's historic sites.

http://www.stateparks.com/pennsylvania_parks_and_recreation_destinations.html

An excellent online guide to Pennsylvania's parks.

Text-Dependent Questions

1. Why did England's king grant William Penn a charter for Pennsylvania?
2. What was the Articles of Confederation? Why was it replaced?
3. What is fracking?

Research Project

Read about the Constitutional Convention of 1787. Write a one-page report summarizing the issues that were debated, or a one-page profile of one of the delegates.

Index

Numbers in **bold italics** refer to captions.

Series Glossary of Key Terms

bicameral—having two legislative chambers (for example, a senate and a house of representatives).

cede—to yield or give up land, usually through a treaty or other formal agreement.

census—an official population count.

constitution—a written document that embodies the rules of a government.

delegation—a group of persons chosen to represent others.

elevation—height above sea level.

legislature—a lawmaking body.

precipitation—rain and snow.

term limit—a legal restriction on how many consecutive terms an office holder may serve.